No Chance Encounter

No Chance Encounter

Meeting Yourself in Others

Kay Pollak

FINDHORN
Press

© Kay Pollak 1994
First published in Sweden as *Att Växa Genom Möten*
English edition first published 1996 © Findhorn Press
Second printing 1998
ISBN 1 899171 46 0

Translated from the original Swedish by Britt & Philip Gaut,
Dances with Words, Mill House, Cholsey, Wallingford,
Oxfordshire, England

British Library Cataloguing-in-Publication Data.
A catalogue record for this book is available from
the British Library.

Set in Palatino by Findhorn Press
Cover design by David Gregson

Printed and bound by WSOY, Finland

Published by
Findhorn Press
The Park, Findhorn,
Forres IV36 0TZ
Scotland
tel +44 (0)1309 690582/fax 690036
e-mail thierry@findhorn.org
http://www.findhorn.org/findhornpress/

A big thank you to Carin who encouraged me to write this book and who so many times helped me find the words — for what I really wanted to say.

Contents

Part 2
More Ideas to Put Into Practice

Part 3
'The Graduate Course'

To the reader

Nothing in this course is new to you.

You are already familiar with everything in this book.

It is about meeting other people and growing as an adult — through your encounters with other people.

It is aimed at everyone who meets and works with others. Indeed, anyone who wants to gain self-knowledge and to grow through meeting other people will find this book useful.

It is my wish that you, your family, friends and colleagues at work will find this book valuable in your daily lives. I hope the exercises will enrich you and contribute to a better interpersonal climate.

It is perhaps the shortest course there is on how — in a new and personal way — you can get involved in creating an improved environment for yourself and the people you meet, and on what you can do to feel better and to be more in touch with yourself and others.

The book is in three parts. Part 3 has just eleven pages. I call it 'the graduate course'.

Read the book.
Read carefully. Take it easy.
Read and live with the contents.
Read again. Discuss with others.
Rejoice at your progress.
And slowly, gently, let change begin!

I wish you all the best.

Part One
No Chance Encounter

Everyone I meet is my teacher

I have found this to be absolutely true.

I have something to learn from everyone I meet.

Can you point to a single person of your acquaintance from whom you have nothing to learn?

In my relationships with others this basic outlook is liberating. I have something to learn from every encounter with another person!

With this attitude each encounter becomes more exciting, rewarding and enjoyable — for both parties.

Try reading this thought silently now and then:

In every encounter with another person I have something to learn.

A very exciting thought

Imagine that no encounter between people is coinciden-tal. Imagine that everyone I meet is sent for a purpose!

When first I came across this idea my reaction was one of doubt. Impossible, I thought. Who could possibly arrange all the meetings?

But gradually I began to try out the idea. And in a remark-able and tangible way it became more rewarding to start going through life with that very thought.

A number of encounters, both with people I knew and with strangers, became more exciting. Sometimes almost intoxicating! I can't say that the thought is with me con-stantly, but:

Just imagine if everyone I meet is sent for a purpose.

I begin to think and believe it is so. Life becomes more fun and more meaningful with such a thought.

If you look back over your own life, you can see that every person you have ever met — every single one — has con-tributed in their own way to your becoming just who you are today. No one else has ever featured in your life other than those you have come to meet in various ways. Just them and nobody else.

Why not try out the thought? Take it easy. Live with it for a while.

Just imagine . . . everyone I meet is sent for a purpose.

Read carefully:

I can and I will learn from other people.

They are all sent for me to practise with.

Projection

Instead of seeing ourselves, we often blame others.

This is called projection. We project onto others the problems we have within ourselves. We transfer our own problems onto those who are quite innocent. In so doing we avoid looking at ourselves. We have all done this in tight situations. And we all have, more or less, been subjects of adult projection when we were children.

Example: When an adult is under stress because of his or her own problems, a child might hear: *'How whining and tiresome you are! Stop being so awkward.'*

This is an example of projection — transferring your own problem — onto someone who is totally innocent.

This is how many of us were treated as children. Adults loaded their own problems onto us.

And so it was that most of us learned how simple it can be to 'solve' life's problems — by putting the blame for our own problem onto somebody else. This, of course, is hardly constructive.

Find ways of talking openly about projections with your friends and colleagues.

What should you do when you notice that you are projecting?

The first step, surely, you have already taken! The first step is seeing and knowing that you are doing it.

A next step towards breaking this pattern can be found on the next page.

(While working with this book, I sometimes thought that the next page was the most important one in the entire book.)

A powerful insight

I am not upset for the reason I think.

It surely happens that you get upset, disturbed and irritated. Next time you get upset, angry, disturbed or irritated about somebody near you, step aside and tell yourself:

I am not upset for the reason I think.
(This concept is from the book *A Course in Miracles*.)

It is sometimes difficult to see this. Most of us are taught to think that it is 'they' who are the cause of our feeling the way we do.

We don't really want to see ourselves as co-creators of what is going on — co-creators and responsible — because we are disturbed, irritated and feeling bad. We don't want to find the reason for being irritated within ourselves! It is often easier to think and believe that if only 'they' were different, then everything would be better. It is often easier to put the blame on others (projection).

So, try it. Next time you are upset, furious, disturbed or irritated about somebody, try thinking to yourself:

I am not upset for the reason I think.

This sentence works like a spanner. It opens up the possibility of seeing yourself instead of blaming others.

Once you have found one such example for yourself — truly feeling it to be relevant — then quite soon you will find more of them . . .

And when you can become aware of this once in a while, then you can take giant leaps in your personal development — and you will feel much better.

Find examples of your own!

An absolute truth

Remind yourself now and again:

I alone am responsible for how I choose to interpret what I see.

I am responsible for how I choose to interpret what I see. That is obvious. Nobody else but me is responsible for how I choose to interpret what I see.

Example: You are in a meeting at work and you are addressing the others. Suddenly you notice that one of them is yawning. It's up to you how you choose to interpret this. If your self-confidence is low, you may instantly choose to interpret the yawn as an expression of low estimation of you. Maybe you get nervous. Perhaps you think: *'I'm no good! I'm not good enough!'*

You interpret the yawn as an attack on yourself.

You become a victim of your own interpretation of reality. Knowing nothing about the yawner, or what sort of night he or she may have had, you allow them to determine your feelings.

Remind yourself often:

Reality and my conception of reality are not identical.

There are other ways of seeing and interpreting.

If you are feeling fine and have a good self-image and good self-confidence, you may choose to see things differently. Maybe you will think: *'Perhaps he had a sleepless night? Wonderful that he came at all!'* Or: *'Someone's yawning. Maybe the air is stale in here.'*

You can make different choices.

You realise that each choice you make shows how you value yourself.

Each choice you make is an evaluation of yourself!

Often think the thought:

I alone am responsible for how I choose to interpret what I see.

'You are no good'

Read this and think about it: A sociological investigation in America concerned a group of three-year-olds. Each child was equipped with a tape-recorder that ran for hours. Every audible message was recorded over a period of two weeks. All the cassettes were then collected and the researchers started analysing and classifying the messages these children received. They found that 85% of the messages included the words 'stop', 'no' or 'don't'. But above all: *85% of the messages contained the fundamental evaluation: 'You are not good enough. You are not OK as you are. You are not good enough. You are no good.'*

It's good to know this — that many of us have had this 'personal law' imprinted on us, more or less, in thousands of different ways, and that this personal law (which is a lie) is the reason why we often misinterpret reality. We create pictures of reality that are untrue.

Reading about this can, naturally, feel like hard work. We are reminded of the fact that we have not always been able to be the 'world's greatest' with children.

It brings up feelings of guilt. Indeed, you may feel like throwing this book away.

In that case, try this amusing thought:

The only true thing one can say about the past is that it no longer exists.

It is never too late to try again!
We are here to learn.

Your True Self

Deep within you is all that is perfect.
Deep within you is the one you were meant to be.

Your True Self is always there within you.
Everyone has his or her 'True Self'. Each one of us.

Your True Self can be locked up.
But it can never be completely extinguished.
There is always a yearning for your True Self.
This longing is there in all our hearts.
That is a reason for hope.

And you know exactly when you are in touch
with your True Self.
Maybe it happened for just ten minutes yesterday.
But still. You know.
You were in touch with another human being
totally without fear.
You were in touch with yourself as you were meant to be.
A moment of happiness, power and total presence.
It is dancing with 'the best in yourself'.

'Not-free' time

As children we often heard: *'You mustn't'* . . . *'Don't make a mess'* . . . *'Don't put your shoes there!'* . . . *'Don't miss the bus!'* . . . *etc.*

There was no end to negations and prohibitions — many, many don'ts!

How do we adults talk to each other?

Here is an amusing exercise for you if you work with people.

Decide in your group that during a short, limited time each day for a week you will talk without using the words 'not' or 'don't'.

Example: Each day between twenty to ten and ten o'clock (just 20 minutes to start with!) all communication should happen without using the word 'not'. You will have fun. You'll have a good laugh at each other's crazy paraphrasing.

You need a lot of concentration to begin with.

So, decide on a 'not-free' time of the day. A few weeks later you might add another period later in the afternoon. And then you can expand these periods. Talk without using the word 'not'. You will notice differences. You will feel better.

Note that I'm not saying it is wrong or forbidden to use the word 'not'. What I am saying is that wonderful things start happening in and around you when you economise on that word — when you try other ways of expressing yourself. And it's fun. You will get better and better at it. Give it a go!

Positive pictures

It is useful to know that sentences including 'don'ts' influence us in a quite definite way.

Here is an example concerning a child. The example is good because it's so obvious. If you work with adults, you will find similar examples.

Example: You are with a child of about four or five who is learning to ride a bike. You are standing on a small, rough path. A short way ahead of you, slightly to one side, there is a hole in the path. You are standing behind the child holding on to the saddle and are about to let go. You shout in the child's ear: **'Don't ride into the hole over there! You can see there's a hole in front of you! For heaven's sake,** *don't* **ride that way!'**

You let go of the bike and the child wobbles — BOOM! Straight into the hole! And after you gave such a clear warning!

Can we understand how this could happen? Yes, of course we can.

Our subconscious mind doesn't take in the word 'not'.

Our subconscious only takes in — understands — pictures.

Our subconscious works in pictures. When you say, **'Don't ride into the hole!'** what sort of image does the child's subconscious create?

Within the child a picture of riding down into the hole is formed. The subconscious steers the muscles. **The message to the child's subconscious says 'Ride into the hole!'** There is no picture of 'not riding into the hole'.

It would, perhaps, be better to say: **'I'll let go soon. You'll be riding in the middle of the path. You'll ride safely straight ahead. Good luck!'**

The positive picture is always there.

Practise and help each other to give and create 'illuminating' pictures like this. They create a sense of joy and are easier to grasp. The subconscious is filled with powerful and affirmative images which will colour everything.

As I said, you will laugh at all the curious rephrasing that you will be forced into. Then you will suddenly discover that you are naturally communicating in positive and constructive target pictures. And feeling all the better for it. Those around you will experience the benefit too.

Seek out the good

Have you sometimes felt that it's very difficult to change your behaviour towards a certain person? I have felt like that, anyway. Thousands of times you can decide in your own mind: 'Tomorrow I'll be fair to Smith and cope with him much better.' But all the same, for various reasons, you so easily fall back into the same old pattern, and then feel like a failure again. You try to change your behaviour — and fail. You want to do good, but can't seem to manage it.

The following is something that has become true for me:

The only thing I can change is my own thinking.

It is on the level of thoughts that all change originates. It is on the level of thoughts that I make my choices.

Here is a fantastic exercise that really can help you change your thoughts:

Sit for a while in peace and quiet. Relax. Close your eyes. Breathe deeply. Feel the serenity in your body.

Choose one person whom you sometimes feel is difficult for you. Picture that person in your mind.

Sit quietly picturing this person in your mind's eye. Maintain contact with the good within yourself.

Focus your thoughts on one single positive feature of this person. Take your time until you can find this positive aspect, even though it may be difficult. You will find something.

When you have found one good thing about this person, then *see* (visualise) this feature in him or her. Really spend time on this. Picture the person in front of you with this particular quality. Totally.

Picture different situations where this quality stands out in this person. And feel the amazing change in your body. Notice what's happening inside yourself.

You become happy when you think positive things about another person!

Carry on. Find another positive thing about this person. Repeat the procedure. Feel how these thoughts affect you.

Feel the peace in your body, in your face.

One thing is for sure — *you will behave differently next time you meet this person.*

Thoughts are creative

Whatever I expect in another human being, I will look for and find. What I want to see — that I will see.

My thoughts about another person are creative. What I think about somebody tends very easily to become reality. When I expect something of someone, I see to it — in various ways — that it becomes manifest. This is called the Pygmalion effect.

The Pygmalion effect: *Whatever I think about somebody — it turns out to be true, so I'm right. Whatever I think about somebody — it proves to be so, and I'm not wrong. I need never have any doubts.*

Then I become a person living in a world where whatever I think about others *is* so. I become someone who looks for all the things in others that will prove me 'right'.

My thoughts are creative.

Furthermore, other people with whom I have contact feel and know what I expect of them, and often act to fulfil my expectations.

If I think of somebody, 'That's a tiresome person,' then he or she easily and often quite unconsciously will prove me right by becoming 'tiresome'.

The fantastic bit is that I can change my thoughts about anybody!

Remind yourself of the fact that you and you alone think your thoughts. Tell yourself now and again during the day:

I am responsible for my own thoughts.

Think from time to time:

I can change my thoughts about myself.

I can change my thoughts about other people.

This is undeniably true and actually revolutionary. You can change your thoughts.

You can change your thoughts about another person.

You can change your thoughts about yourself.

Good rumours

One way of helping each other is to spread good rumours about each other. Increase the good 'thought mass' that surrounds all of us. Take part in it. Work at it.

Circulate rumours of what is good. Circulate good rumours!

And do it so that you yourself will feel better. Yes, I really mean that. Do it so that you can feel better yourself. Try it.

Circulate good rumours about colleagues, patients, customers, clients, pupils . . . Talk a lot and often about what is true and good! This is a way to transform the world. At the same time you will experience the joy of keeping company with good thoughts.

A group that is rid of backbiting becomes more secure and happier. The more secure the group, the better it will work. It will also have a greater sense of purpose.

Everybody longs to feel a sense of purpose.

A better working environment

Create positive patterns. Break the negative ones!

Here is a constructive method that you can follow in order to improve the atmosphere where you work:

- Decide that you want to change the atmosphere.

- Decide that you will commit yourself to this. Don't tell anybody what you are up to.

- Choose a calm place at home, sit down in peace and quiet, and focus your thoughts on one person. It can be a person you dislike and to whom you now want to change your relationship. Or it can be a colleague, patient or pupil that you don't get on well with and with whom you would like to improve things. Let's call this person 'X'.

- Make a list of X's positive qualities. Find things that you *truly, sincerely* can say X is good at. Write these down. Make it neat and beautiful. Each item on the list is something you honestly think about X. You may come to see and hear lots of negative things about X, but you will pay no attention to them now. You don't deny them, but you are concentrating on other things at the moment. You are focusing only on the positive.

- Once you have your list of X's positive qualities, you will find there are things that you can appreciate and even admire and be grateful for in this person.

  NOW CHOOSE ONE ITEM from your list.

Think about this thing and then . . . one day at work in some context . . . when X isn't present . . . you will say to somebody:

'You know, I think X is fantastic at . . .'
What you say must be a sincere feeling.

If the person you speak to reacts negatively, DON'T RESPOND. Just let it be. Release it.

If you like, you can repeat your 'good rumour' some other time to another colleague.

Some days later you can choose another good quality from your list, 'dropping' it casually to one or more people . . . and so on.

Try this, and you will experience a miracle!

A reminder

My thoughts about another human being are often more about what is inside me than about what is inside that other person.

What I think about another human being says more about me than it says about that other person.

This text can act as a reminder:

**What Peter thinks about Paul
often says more about Peter
than it does about Paul.**

Why not put this text up on the wall at work?

Or if you want to reformulate it like this:

**What I think about Peter
says more about myself
than it says about Peter.**

Or maybe say it like this:

**It is in my mind
that my thoughts are created.**

**My thoughts about you
show something about me.**

**My thoughts about you
say nothing about you.**

About true and false thoughts

Think of someone you know. Immediately you will have a thought about that person. It's instantaneous.

What if every thought you have about another human being either increases the truth about him or her, or increases the lie — the image, the illusion, the fantasy — about that person?

What if there are no neutral thoughts about other people? For me this has become a truth.

Read often:

Every thought I have adds either to the truth or to the illusion.

Every thought I have either increases the truth or increases the lie.

Example: You are sitting on the bus on your way home from work. You are looking at somebody. You get a thought in your head about them. Either that thought will increase the 'true-thought mass' about this other human being, or otherwise it will increase the lie — image, illusions, fantasies — about this person.

Once you have realised this you will start paying attention to your thoughts. It is not unexciting!

Remind yourself often that nobody else thinks your thoughts. You alone are responsible for your thoughts.

Tell yourself quietly now and then during the day:

I am responsible for my thoughts.

Naturally, anything you say about a person also increases either the truth or the lie about him or her. But, for now, start by practising how to pay attention to your thoughts. Because it is only at this level that you can make a choice. So tell yourself quietly now and then during the day:

Each thought I have about another human being increases either the truth or the lie about that person.

And read this too:

I am responsible for my thoughts.

Seven golden words

The following exercise may be the funniest that you feel you can handle.

Next time you feel criticised, put upon or attacked by a colleague, patient, customer, client, pupil, your teenage son or daughter . . . try these Seven Golden Words.

Take a deep breath and say calmly, on the out-breath, to that person:

There is something in what you say.

You will experience a miracle. It will be a relief, for both of you!

The very best opportunities to practise this often come from the person you have chosen to live with. You have chosen him or her so you can get really good lessons! In your relationship as a couple, sometimes days will pass while you have to take deep breaths before you can actually get around to saying, calmly on an out-breath: *'There is something in what you say.'*

Practise and practise. Gradually you will be able to start accepting the ancient truth:

> *You cannot change another human being.*
> *The only one you can change is yourself.*

Seeing the truth

Next time you meet someone who is irritated, or furious, or perhaps arrogant, ironic, fault-finding or out of balance, then remind yourself calmly:

A person who is feeling well never has any need to attack or ridicule anybody else.

Don't say it to this other person! Keep it to yourself and you will start to see him or her in a new light.

You will not so readily feel threatened in the same old way. You won't get hurt so easily. You won't return the anger so quickly. You will be able to remain calmer. Your heart will beat easier.

Before you stands a person who isn't feeling well right now.

If you can see this, you will probably act and react in a way that will make the other person feel better — and you too. You will get better results from the encounter. If you become caught up in the old pattern — starting to blame this person — you will feel worse yourself (and, naturally, so will the affected person).

So, next time you meet someone you find disturbed, arrogant, aggressive . . . try it .

A quarrel never starts with the first utterance.
It starts with the second.

I have something to learn

Next time you are disturbed, irritated, furious, exhausted and tired of a colleague (patient, customer, pupil, partner . . .) try to say carefully to yourself (this will demand great willingness on your part):

What is happening right now is happening because I have something to learn.

I'm not saying this is easy. But when we blame others for something that's going on, we may be transferring — projecting — our own problem onto an innocent person.

It is my choice and nobody else's whether I want to transfer my irritation to another human being, or whether I want to see and find the reasons for it within myself. Whether I want to learn something — about myself — and grow.

Example: I used to get irritated and off balance if people came too late when I was giving talks. I really became a victim of how I chose to interpret reality.

Finally, I was able to see that *'I wasn't upset or irritated for the reasons I thought I was'* about people coming too late. No!

I confused cause and effect. The problem wasn't 'them'. The reason for my irritation was wholly within me. The problem was mine alone. The reason was my attitude.

The truth was that I had a poor self-image and was very afraid of losing control. I was afraid!

At first I dared not see that fear. It was more convenient and easier to see the others as a reason for my disturbance, rather than see the reason for the problem within myself.

I had a lot to learn.

So, next time you are disturbed and irritated at somebody, try stepping aside and telling yourself calmly:

What is happening right now is happening because
I have something to learn.

There is hope

What has become true for me is that:

**When I condemn someone else
I am not seeing the whole person.**

Deep down everybody knows this.

I'm not saying it is easy. But it is true that each time I condemn somebody, I'm not seeing the whole of that person. I'm only looking at a miserably small fragment of him or her.

If I get a chance to see the whole person, their entire life history, all their sufferings, misfortunes, dreams and endeavours, then I would become unable to condemn and scoff. I can dislike and condemn somebody's actions, but I will be open to that person and understand once I get a chance to see the whole. It is remarkable, but true.

To see the whole is sometimes the hardest thing. It is so easy to see and focus on a small, limited part and to condemn.

All of this really gives a reason for hope — it is simple and self-evident. But somehow it is still difficult to see and apply it.

Prejudging others

This is about my health:

When I belittle or prejudge another person, child or adult, I am actually harming myself.

I weaken myself by condemning others. I lose my enjoyment of life and good spirits. I feel awful. My immune capacity diminishes. (This can be proved right down to the level of white blood cells.)

When I have belittling and prejudicial thoughts about another person I get trapped in various ways. I find it harder to be totally open to this person. I find it more difficult to look them in the eye in a wonderful and open way. The best of me no longer glows spontaneously towards this person. I start avoiding them. 'Distancing' sets in. I feel rotten and guilty. Deep down I know I am separated from the best of me. This person and I — we never 'get to dance with each other'.

I'm not saying this is easy. I don't say I manage to live without criticising and blaming others. But what I do say is: *It has become true for me, that as I prejudge others I am really harming and weakening myself. Whenever I do this, I myself never feel well.*

A person who has contemptuous thoughts about another human being cannot be a happy person. Everybody knows that.

Everybody gets negative and prejudicial thoughts about others. We all get them. The question is: how do I reflect on these thoughts of mine?

So, if you find yourself accusing and prejudging some-body, picture the pointing hand in your mind.

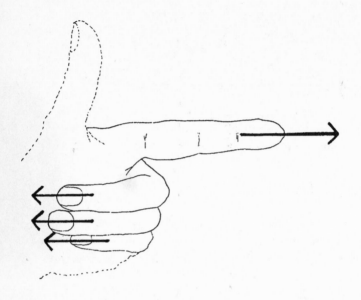

When you are 'pointing a finger' and condemning, accus-ing and blaming somebody else, you tend to forget that three fingers are pointing back — at yourself.

Attack — fear

Sometimes we attack other people. What if I'm always going to feel some sort of fear when faced with a person that I have attacked in some way?

For me this has become true:

I will always fear the one I have attacked.

What do I mean by attacking another human being?

Slander, for instance, is an attack. Making derogatory remarks about somebody is an attack. To ridicule and be ironic about somebody is to attack that person. To blame and accuse someone is to attack them, and so on . . .

An attack can also be a thought! To think negative and condemning thoughts about another person is to attack them. When I attack someone, I always create guilt in myself.

My attack will automatically and unconsciously create a fear in me that this other person will in turn attack me . . . which will create (as a sort of defence) further attacking on my part . . . which in turn will increase my sense of guilt . . . which will create new fear of attack from this other person . . . and so on.

It is all an unconscious, growing and accelerating vicious circle.

Within this circle lies the explanation for bullying.

Each attack separates me further from the me I was meant to be.

I will always fear the one I have attacked.

You will realise that this is so if you study yourself in

your everyday life. Notice when you feel free and when you feel unfree.

Maybe some people believe that they are responsible only for their actions — for what they actually do — and not for what they think. This is how I used to think.

The truth is that I am responsible for what I think.

Example: You enter a room where several people are waiting. It is some form of meeting and you are to address it. Maybe you are about to give a talk. Suddenly, seemingly without reason, you get an instant negative and condemning thought about somebody present in the room. Perhaps the thought goes something like: *'Good heavens! Help! Is he here?'* or *'Oh no! She's here too!'*

Then things get difficult. You have attacked another person. Deep down within you, unconsciously, you will be waiting for an attack from that person. You will feel fear. You will become defensive. You will stand confined in the room. It will not be easy to 'dance' with the best in yourself.

Above all, the best in you will not shine warmly and openly towards this person. You will start avoiding him or her. You are no longer free. A fear of this other person has emerged. You are aware of all of this in the room — and in your own body.

It takes a lot of energy to control all of this. You will probably be tense and tired afterwards.

To embrace calmly the meaning of *'I will always fear the person I have attacked'* is revolutionary. In the final reckoning, it is all about my own health.

Being enlightened

We probably know, deep down, that when we have negative, judgemental and ridiculing thoughts about someone else, this really says something about ourselves.

Behind every negative thought I have about another person lurks some form of fear within myself.

Could it really be that when I have a judgemental thought about somebody, that person in fact reminds me of an aspect of myself that I don't want to look at — something that I fear in myself. He or she reminds me of part of myself that I am strongly denying and suppressing.

Sometimes people say (as a sort of psychological axiom) that:

> **What I deny and suppress in myself**
> **I tend to scoff at and attack outside myself.**

To know about this human 'law', and really be able to see how it operates in myself, is the most important condition of being 'enlightened'.

I have tried many times to avoid seeing myself. I have believed (and been certain) that my frustration, disturbance and imbalance are caused by 'them'. Then I have projected the reason for my feeling bad onto the other person — always through some form of attack. I make someone else the scapegoat, to avoid seeing something in myself. That, of course, is hardly constructive.

Each such attack is an attempt to avoid seeing myself.

Each such attack, in thought, word or deed, is a form of defence. The aim is to avoid seeing myself.

Surely, when it is easy for me to accept myself, it becomes easier to accept others too.

What if, when I'm busy condemning or attacking another person, I'm really speaking, in a unique way, about myself?

Through my condemnation of others I reveal a lot about myself.

My thoughts about me

We have said that thoughts are creative.

And that the thoughts I have about another person tend easily to become reality.

In the same way, what I think about myself also easily becomes reality.

Each thought I have creates a memory in my cells.

If in the morning I think, 'Today will be a difficult day,' the day tends to be just that. My subconscious gets charged with negative images through having thoughts like that — negative expectations. My subconscious steers me and wants to be right. My subconscious therefore sees to it that I get it 'right'.

The day will be difficult!

And I can say to myself: 'What did I tell you?'

If, instead, in the morning I choose to visualise quite different images, filling myself with wonderful and positive pictures of myself in various situations, the day will turn out to be much more like those images.

In this sense my thoughts about myself are creative.

Read carefully:

Each thought I have creates a memory in my cells.

I can choose which thoughts I have about myself.

I alone am responsible for my thoughts.

Anger

Anger is a very loaded subject.

I'm not saying that I never get angry. I'm not saying that anger is an 'ugly' emotion.

There are no emotions that are 'nobler' or 'better' than others. In fact, there is no right and wrong about emotions. Emotions are what they are — emotions.

Anger is an emotion — just as OK as any other emotion.

The question is: what am I *doing* with my anger?

I have noticed myself that when I'm furious at somebody, often I'm really projecting my anger onto an innocent person. It has never been constructive.

When we feel anger we are seldom level-headed and conscious of what we are really furious about.

What if it is like this:

All anger is an attempt to make someone else feel guilty.

What if that is really how it is? Try the thought! Think for a moment about a recent instance when you were really furious with someone.

Anger — fear

Next time you meet somebody who is really furious, angry and upset . . .

. . . ask yourself:

What is this person so afraid of?

Behind all anger there is some form of fear. Don't say it aloud! Just ask yourself silently: *'What is this person so afraid of?'*

And you will see a different person in front of you. Your empathy can be awakened. Behind the anger there is always fear.

Behind the anger there is always a person crying out for help. All anger is really a desperate cry for help.

All shouts of fury and anger are examples of impotence. We shout only when we don't understand our own fury.

All violence is an expression of impotence. We hit out only when we don't understand our own anger.

When I yell at somebody and refuse to listen (don't have the strength to listen) I'm doing it to silence something within myself which I don't want to see (don't have the strength to see) at that moment.

Behind all anger there is always some form of fear.

Surely it is a fact that the most aggressive people are always the most frightened. Much of history would, naturally, look different if the most aggressive people had thought more often: *'What is it that I don't have the courage to see within myself?'*

So, next time you meet somebody who is so furious, angry

and upset that he or she is trembling, try asking yourself calmly:

What is this person so afraid of?

Practise and practise.

Really seeing

All fear is a cry for help.

If I am afraid, I may put on a mask — a 'false' expression — as protection. Like some sort of armour. We all do it from time to time in order to survive in different situations. Every mask you see is some kind of shield.

Example: You see a boy looking tough and nonchalant crossing the dance floor. You see the mask, the veil — there to conceal his insecurity, his fear. Within the boy a restless heart is thumping. But he doesn't want to show it. He protects himself by putting on a 'tough' show — a mask. A kind of armour. This mask is his 'false' expression. His shield.

From this simple example you can see: **Each mask is a defence, an entreaty — a cry — for help.** If you can see that, then you will see the truth. **That is really seeing.**

But if you react to the mask and the tough attitude with fear or contempt or even downright admiration, then you are reacting to something that is 'false'. You are not seeing the truth. **You are the victim of a misinterpretation.**

It is also obvious that it is you who choose how to interpret what you see. It is you who choose if you want to see the truth when you look at the boy or if you want to react to his mask — the falseness.

Whenever you see the 'false' in an encounter without accepting it as true, you become a potential helper, a liberator.

The bigger the mask you see, the greater is the cry for help.

An exercise

We can learn a lot by practising seeing clear, extreme examples. They exist so that we will learn to see.

You see a 'skinhead' approaching: grim face, shaven head, black boots, clacking heel-plates. He has a death's-head for an ear-ring. What do you see? What do you feel?

Do you react to the veil, the mask, 'the false'? Do you shrink and run away? Or can you see the signals that cry for help and beg for love?

Perhaps you become fearful, distance yourself, tense up, stiffen, look down at the pavement as you pass. You will not be someone who looks him in the eye. Maybe you even have feelings of contempt. In that case you are a victim of this boy's mask.

You see the 'false' and accept it as truth.

The truth in this case is clear: There goes a young man who is asking for help, who is crying out for love. Every aspect of his being, face and clothes is an appeal for help. All skinheads are crying: Love me!

He sees you and, naturally, feels your fear. Your contempt too, perhaps.

Your own misinterpretation distances and separates you.

See the truth (in this case it is very obvious) and you can choose other feelings. Maybe you feel like stopping, or at least giving him the gift of seeing him. There he is in front of you, crying, appealing, beseeching. Nobody taught him to say the words: *'Love me — accept me!'*

When he was small and, in the various ways of a child,

tried to express this need — yes, appealed for this basic human right to love and acceptance — perhaps he was rejected, ridiculed, scorned or laughed at. Or left to feel lonely. Punishments of different kinds.

What streams of lava there are inside him! What pain! And he learned to conceal it with this mask of chill and bravado. With this 'false' expression.

We all carry within us the need to receive love. It is a real need.

A poem

What we came close to on the previous page is so superbly
illustrated in the lines of this poem:

We want to be loved
Failing that, admired
Failing that, feared
Failing that, hated and despised.

We want to arouse in others some sort of emotion.
The soul shivers before the void and wants contact
whatever the price.

From 'Dr. Glas'
by the Swedish poet Hjalmar Söderberg

You have now read Part One.

Take a break.

Have a rest. Take it easy.

Choose to advance slowly.

Try to look with excitement and curiosity on what there is still to learn. We are now about halfway through the course.

Meanwhile, ponder now and then what you think Shakespeare may have been thinking when he wrote:

There is nothing good or bad,
but thinking makes it so.

Part Two

More Ideas to Put Into Practice

Look within

A simple reminder:

Next time you are upset with your partner, your colleague or a client.

You are so angry that you are trembling. You are shouting silly things.

Instead of shouting:

'You're an idiot! I hate you! You're driving me mad!'

try to formulate something like:

'It feels like I'm going mad — where inside me is it coming from?'

Or try to find words along the lines of:

'You stir something within me . . . you remind me of something that makes me tremble with anger . . . and that's strange . . . I wonder where that comes from?'

Do try to say:

*'I'm really furious — but rest assured that it has **nothing** to do with you.'*

You back off. You don't subject the other person to your anger. You step to one side and ask yourself: *'Why am I reacting like this? What is this saying about me? What can I do about it? What is being awakened in me?'*

It's a good idea to look again at the most fundamental sentence from the beginning of Part One, the 'spanner' that helps you make this shift — from projection to seeing inwards to yourself:

I am not upset for the reason I think.

An exercise

Look around you. Think about your reactions to different people. Can you see the truth about them? Or are you the victim of your own interpretations?

Example: You have a colleague who is ironic, cynical and arrogant. Maybe you are frightened of him. Perhaps you feel disgust and contempt. You react strongly to the signals he sends out. You react by distancing yourself from his 'ice-cold and nonchalant' body language. You draw back. Lower your eyes. You are no longer in touch with the best in yourself — you are no longer what you were meant to be.

You are the victim of another person's signals.

You have made yourself smaller. Weaker. You are the victim of your own interpretation of his ways. You see and react to what is 'false'. You see and react to the mask that he is holding up as a shield.

Read again:

I alone am responsible for how I choose to interpret what I see.

You are not seeing the truth about this man. Irony and arrogance are always expressions of fear.

The truth is that his irony and arrogance are messages to you about *his* fear. They are his defence. They are the mask — the game he is playing — the defence he is erecting. He once learned (maybe as a child) to use them each time he felt uncertain. In order to survive. Everything you see is a cry for help, an appeal, his prayer for help: 'Love me!'

You see it! Your new outlook has begun to work. It's easy in a case as clear as this.

Many are the opportunities to practise seeing the truth. Sometimes you will fail. You will feel reserved and dwarfed. You will feel envy and anger, disgust and contempt because of how somebody is. Life is full of opportunities to practise. See everything as a lesson! See life as a school for practice.

All the fear you see is a cry for help.

Behind every mask you see lies the truth about that person. And the greater the mask, the greater is the cry for help.

Try this sentence out now and then in your everyday life:

I am committed to looking at things and people in a quite new and different way. I want to see the truth.

Read to yourself: *'I no longer want to be a victim of the pictures that I myself interpret wrongly. I know that all masks are there to conceal fear. I know that masks are cries for help. Appeals for love. I know this to be so. I want to see.'*

Your shift happens at the moment you see one single phenomenon in a new and different way. Once you have done it, you will do it again . . . and again. There is hope.

*Now there follow
three items
about intrusions . . .*

Slander — 1

You are having a break in the coffee room at work. At the same table one of your colleagues, A, is making slander-ous remarks about another colleague, B, who is not pre-sent. You hear what is being said. Maybe you mutter, 'Is that so?' a few times and laugh with embarrassment. You don't really feel you are taking part. Perhaps you mum-ble an 'Indeed!' or an almost inaudible 'Well, well!' You sip your coffee. Your colleague continues his or her incred-ible description of B. You really think you are not partic-ipating at all. You neither agree nor disagree.

Then the break is over. Your colleague rushes off. You drain your cup, get up and walk out into the corridor. It's a long one. From the other end of the corridor B is now walking towards you. Help! Luckily you happen to be next to the toilets, so you quickly dive into one. You hear B walk past.

Suppose that you have silently taken part in an attack on B? Can it be that you too have attacked B through your silent participation?

How would it be if silent participation always creates a feeling of guilt in you?

You really feel guilty when you meet B. Consciously or unconsciously. And from now on there is something between you and B. You are no longer a free person. You will perhaps start avoiding B in different ways. Maybe from now on you will not so easily meet B with the warmest and most open eyes.

It is tragic. Not only for B, but also for you.

Unless you do something about it!

You feel there is truth in the saying:

I will always fear the one I have attacked.

When I attack someone I harm myself.

BUT WHAT DO YOU DO WHEN THIS HAPPENS?

On the next page you will find an excellent piece of advice.

Slander — 2

Here is an excellent piece of advice if you ever find yourself in a situation where somebody starts speaking ill of a person who is not present.

Next time you are exposed to person A speaking negatively and judgementally about person B who is not present, try this:

While A goes on and on slandering the absent B, you focus all your thought-energy on finding something positive about B. You search your memory for one of B's good qualities: pleasant manners, something positive that B has done, a special ability that B has . . .

Look for and find *one* positive thing about B. Something that you really and truly can say is good and worth appreciating. When you have found it, say it calmly to A.

And you help to change the world!

Don't get into an argument. Just say this one good thing and you will witness a remarkable change in A's face. It will do you a world of good. And it will do B a world of good. And, strangely enough, it will do A a world of good too.

You will be able to meet B and look him or her straight in the eye next time your paths cross.

Sitting quietly participating when A is busy slandering B is no different from taking part in a sort of rape of B.

Yes, it is a strong word.

But it is an invasion of someone who is totally defenceless.

Slander — 3

One more piece of advice — if you want to be free:

If A comes up to you and 'confidingly' leans towards you saying: *'I'll tell you something about B. But promise not to say anything to anybody. Promise!'*

First take a deep breath. (Your very life is at stake here.) Take a further breath and then tell A not to say it.

Say that you don't want to hear it.

To listen to and accept this kind of 'confidence' means that in a way you yourself are subjected to an intrusion.

If you choose to listen to A, you will feel guilty and find it hard to be free with B from then on. Separation between you and B may set in.

Take care of yourself. Protect yourself.

To paraphrase an old English proverb:

Lies thrive on eager ears.

One heart at a time

Peace doesn't begin somewhere far away.

Peace doesn't begin with the others putting down their weapons.

Peace doesn't begin when all the others change.

Peace begins here, within.

Peace is achieved through one heart at a time.

Begin with yourself. Continue with your children and your partner.

Go on with other people who, at random it seems, turn up — sent to you on your journey through life.

The world changes when I change my conception of the world.

What I can change is how I understand the world. What I can change is how I interpret other people and how I interpret myself.

Take one heart at a time. The world has changed when I have changed.

There is real hope.

Guilt — a message

Guilt creates projection.

Projection is when we transfer guilt onto others instead of seeing ourselves and our own part in it.

A guilt-laden mind protects itself with projections.
A guilt-laden mind looks for scapegoats.

For me, the contents of these two sentences are true. They are fundamental — basic — for understanding ourselves and what is happening outside us and between people.

Projection is always some form of attack. Each attack on another person creates a feeling of guilt inside me.

To lighten my burden of guilt, I project my problems onto somebody else . . . which creates new guilt, which creates new projections . . . which creates new guilt . . . in an ever-accelerating circle . . .

I have also become convinced that:

Guilt always demands some sort of punishment.

We punish ourselves or somebody else when we feel guilty.

❄

Guilt is a word with a strong religious charge. For many people the word guilt is connected with words like *purgatory, hell and God's punishment.*

There is comfort in knowing that none of this exists!

I see the charged word of guilt like this: *Guilt is a message in my body — a tension that tells me I am separated from my True Self . . . the one I was meant to be.*

Try seeing guilt as a message to yourself.

Two different worlds

We often think it is the external world that determines what we see, understand and perceive. Actually it is my own thoughts that determine what I see.

You could say:

My thoughts guide what I see.

Thoughts of hopelessness show me a hopeless world, while thoughts full of hope show me a hopeful world.

Fearful thoughts show me a world full of enemies, dangers, obstacles and threats.

Loving thoughts show me a different sort of world.

Loving thoughts help me to see not only a world full of love but also a world full of appeals for love, that is to say cries for help.

Loving thoughts help me see the truth. Fearful thoughts create a world of images and illusions.

One person says they see a world full of violence, malice and aggression. Another says that they see a world full of calls for help.

When people see different worlds, they react in different ways. It's an interesting difference.

As soon as I feel fear I tend to rewrite reality, not see the truth.

Just imagine: my 'external reality' is a reflection — a result of — my 'inner reality'.

Practise carefully and calmly absorb:

My experience of reality is not the same as reality.

My fearful thoughts show me a threatening world.

My loving thoughts show me a loving world.

And take this silently within:

I can change my thoughts.

What do I see?

Maybe you have woken up one morning and feel really awful. You are lying in bed thinking: *'Oh no! Not another day.'* You still have your eyes closed. Feet still under the cover.

Slowly you put your feet down on the floor. You are just sitting there . . . holding your head in your hands. *'Oh no! Not another day.'* Then you open your eyes . . . only to see heaps of dust under the bookcase. *'Oh no . . . !'*

You get up, glimpsing an old sock lying on the floor . . . You stumble to the bathroom . . . passing the light switch . . . seeing how dirty the wallpaper is around it.

You enter the bathroom. There's the mirror! You bend down immediately to wash . . . because you can't cope with seeing yourself in the mirror . . .

These are the feelings inside you when you take the bus to work. You look around: *'Oh no! There's one of those kinds of people . . . Ugh!'* At once you turn away. You look around again . . . thinking: *'Most people are too fat . . . And there's one of those pimply ones . . .'*

AND ANOTHER MORNING:

You wake up . . . stretch . . . and are full of:

'Yes! One more day to live!'

You sit on the edge of the bed for a while, looking down at the floor. You still see the wads of dust (but now they resemble interesting cloud formations!) . . . You get up . . . into the bathroom . . . pausing for a while in front of the mirror . . . observing yourself . . . calmly . . . gratefully. What you see is all you have! You are filled with gratitude. And feeling like this you get on the bus, glancing

around: *'Oh, there's that kind of person! How interesting! . . .
Some are rounder than others. That is not unexciting . . . Oh,
and look, there's one of those! Isn't that fantastic! A special person sent for me to practise with.'*

AND THEY ARE THE SAME PEOPLE!

Sometimes you see the fag-ends on the ground. Another
day you see only the birds. It is not with your eyes that
you really see. Your lenses merely let in the light.

Thoughts and feelings steer my seeing.

Choosing thoughts

This is important!

Every thought I have influences my mood and my health.

Negative thoughts weaken me physically and psychologically. Thoughts of gratitude and joy strengthen me physically and psychologically.

We all know this from thousands of our own experiences.

But all the same, it does happen that we sometimes forget. We can slip into *'misery, blame and complaints'* mode. That is human. But we should know that it weakens us.

A lot changes when I start to look consciously at my thoughts and my conversation.

Sometimes you can hear conversations between two or more people that are based solely on *'misery, blame and complaints'*.

It can even seem that the only reason some people meet is to exchange *'misery, blame and complaints'*.

Think of your health!

Practise avoiding such negative conversation.

Rather, choose thoughts of gratitude more often.

On the next page you will find a simple and excellent exercise.

Gratitude

If one day you feel really bad, really ill at ease, lacking in energy and finding everything tedious and boring . . . If one day you feel: *'Oh no! Not another day . . .'*

If you then want to get in touch with better energies, try telling yourself:

> *'One thing that I'm grateful for is . . .'*
> *'Another thing I'm grateful for is . . .'*
> *'One more thing I'm grateful for is . . .'*

Try this one ordinary morning just when you have woken up and you want to feel better and stronger.

For example, you might say:

'One thing I'm grateful for is . . . that I'm healthy. Another thing I'm grateful for is . . . that I have somewhere to live. One more thing I'm grateful for is . . . that there's food in the fridge.' And so on.

What you are doing is, by your own will, focusing your thoughts on something that you can feel gratitude about. Of course, you should focus your thoughts only on what is totally true for you. No false sentiment here.

I am responsible for which thoughts I choose to affect my body. My thoughts can make me feel bad — even make me ill. They can also make me healthier.

It is I who choose my thoughts.

Each thought I have influences every cell in my body.

This 'exercise in gratitude' is excellent to carry out in a working team. Do it from time to time. Let everyone have a say; go around the circle many times. Maybe you should try it when you have had a particularly hard time for some reason. Soon you will be smiling, and then laughing. If you do it together with others it will have more powerful results. Hearing others say what they are grateful for makes you happy. That gives you hope. Try it!

A variation on this exercise, which I have tried myself, goes like this: A team met regularly once a week. The meeting always started with each person saying: *'One new and positive thing since we last met is . . .'*

Guess what sort of energies entered this group!

Optimism

Optimism is seeing every problem as an opportunity.

Next time you have a problem or think you have failed, try this thought:

There is another way of looking at this.

There is always another way of looking at a 'failure'. There is always a kind of opposite to the problem — a kind of opportunity.

To begin with, find one such opportunity. It is a good thing to write it down. Say it to yourself out loud.

Then go on finding more opportunities. Maybe you can write down ten or more opportunities arising from the problem or 'failure' that you find yourself thwarted by.

Soon you will be able see these new opportunities in front of you. Then invest all your energies in the one that is best for you. Here is an example to practise with: You don't get the job that you applied for and so very much wanted.

Opportunities and advantages arising from this event are:
. . . . (try it for yourself)

Optimism is seeing every problem as an opportunity.

I'm not saying it is always easy to think like that. What I do want to say is that:

I alone am responsible for my own life.

To start with, try turning problems into opportunities only in respect to 'little failures' and 'small sorrows'. Soon you will get used to it — and will be able to proceed to more difficult exercises.

Lessons

There are two ways of looking at failures:

One is to consider a failure as a disaster and to keep thinking about it with bitterness. I punish and blame myself. And my thoughts go something like this: *'How silly of me! I'm really stupid. How could I?!'*

Many of us have been brought up and taught to think like that. All such thoughts influence me in a negative way — right down to the cellular level. Try instead saying to yourself:

I can learn from my mistakes in life.

Then a failure turns around to become something wonderful. A lesson!

That is a much more comforting thought. Life is really filled with an endless procession of lessons. We are sitting in the classroom called life, each and every one of us, because we have things to learn. It is only when we don't learn the lesson that a failure can really be called a failure.

One more thing:

Sometimes we think about a period in our life: 'Those years were wasted!' Instead, try carefully thinking this thought:

'Those years were a preparation,
a germination time for what is now.'

Try seeing your 'enemies and misfortunes' as sandpaper in your life.

Read this hopeful sentence often:

I see more today than I saw yesterday.

The picture of me

The picture of myself in life.

All of us carry around pictures of ourselves. Pictures to do with our view of life. Pictures that have been imprinted on us by our parents and grandparents, often from many generations back. We all carry these pictures without being aware of them.

When I attended a course a few years ago I did a visualisation exercise looking for a 'picture of myself in life'.

I'd like to tell you about the picture I perceived.

This was my picture:

A sturdy Ardennes cart-horse is labouring its way up a steep slope. The horse is in harness. It is dragging a huge load of timber over the ground — with no wheels and no snow!

The picture told me something about how I was brought up:

LIFE IS STRUGGLE

I have done many things in my life with that attitude: *Don't give up. It's going to be tough. There will surely be difficulties, obstacles and opposition. But go to it anyway. It's all about struggle.* One is like a fish fighting the ocean.

Life can be exhausting with an outlook like that.

Imagine dancing the tango with such an attitude to life!

But what if it is quite the opposite. What if the rule instead goes like this:

When it is right — then it is light.
When it is light — then it is right.

Find instances in your life when you feel this has been the case.

When it is right it's light,
and when it is light then it's right.

Try carrying that thought with you in your everyday life. Say it to yourself now and again. You will notice the difference.

Really listening

This page and the next one are about the power of personal encounters.

Your ability to listen is probably your most powerful tool for changing those around you.

And also for changing the attitude of those around you to you!

There has been research in which people have tried to measure what is meaningful in communication between people. It has been shown that the words — the speaking itself — often mean as little as seven per cent. Everything else — facial expressions, body language, eyes, the way of listening, and thoughts about the other person — constitutes 93 per cent! All these other things have much greater impact than the words.

Surely you know how it feels when you don't get heard. You have something important to say and the person you are talking to doesn't listen. And you also know how immensely wonderful it is when, for once, you really feel heard. You feel happy — and grateful to the listener.

In life one meets both bad and good listeners.

Try to remember a time when you thought you had something important to say and the person you were talking with was a really poor listener. He or she just didn't listen.

Recall such an incident. You are talking, you have something important to say, and the other person is not listening.

Perhaps they sit looking out the window all the time, or fiddling with a pen, clicking and clicking. They are restless, or they lean back with arms folded. Maybe their whole body is turned away. They are waggling their feet, knitting their brows, sighing and looking at their watch. When the phone rings they are clearly relieved.

In such a situation many of us can feel frustration, anger, paralysis, muteness and total blockage. We may experience feelings of insignificance, grief and loneliness. We may feel insecure, nervous and disturbed. Our heart starts pounding. Suddenly we hear how everything we say sounds disjointed and unintelligible. Everything is wrong. We feel stupid, tired, indifferent. Everything closes in on us in a strange way. We may feel hatred, self-contempt, guilt and a desire for revenge.

Now recall a totally different occasion. Think about when you had something you considered to be important to say, and the person you talked to was a really good listener. He or she really listened — listened to what you were saying.

Recall one such incident. You have something important to say. You are talking and the other person is listening. You have met a good listener!

He or she is there in front of you, relaxed. Looks you in the eye. Looks open, positive and warm. The body is at ease, almost leaning forwards. The head nods as you talk. The hands are resting open. He or she is present. Your listener doesn't interrupt — other than possibly to ask a brief question to ensure that he or she has really understood what you mean.

In such encounters you often feel security and peace. You are filled with warmth, friendship, joy, energy and power. You feel creative. Intelligent. A genius! You gain self-confidence. You become firm and certain. You become trustful, open and childlike. You feel alive, playful, open-handed. Generous! You feel hope, gratitude, responsibility. Many people say they feel love.

This is how we always want to feel.
In touch with the best in us.
As we were meant to be.
All of this we have within us.
All this belongs to our True Self.

A Norwegian girl once told me something very beautiful:

A good listener has eyes you can look into
And a body you can touch — if you want to.

Listen

This is a text that was sent to me anonymously in a letter, and I'd like to share it:

When I ask you to listen to me
and you start giving me good advice,
then you have not done what I asked of you.

When I ask you to listen to me
and you start explaining why I shouldn't feel as I do,
then you are trampling on my feelings.

When I ask you to listen to me
and you think you must do something to sort out my
    problems,
then you fail me, however strange that may sound.

Perhaps that is why praying helps some people.
Because God is mute and doesn't give good advice or
    try to 'fix' things.
He only listens and lets me take care of myself.

So please, just listen to me,
and if you want to say something, be patient.
Then, I promise, I'll listen to you.

Anonymous

Feel free to copy this text.

Leadership

Here is a checklist for all team leaders:

1. Make a list of all your team members stating their positive and strong points; talk often about these — focus on them.

2. Get a good photo of each team member. Look at these pictures often, one at a time, with all your positive thoughts. Your thoughts are creative.

3. Pay attention to your own attitude. Talk about it. Try to change your own attitude. Influence your own thoughts and your collaborators' thoughts. Spread good rumours.

4. Talk frequently about your colleagues' strong points. Say often: **'One thing that I really appreciate about you is . . .'** Leave out the weaker points. Focus on the good things. See the strength rather than the weakness.

5. Expect the best.

6. Picture what each member of the team is in need of. Make a list of each person's particular needs. Satisfy them as much as you can.

7. Create security in the team. The greater the team security, the more you can be yourself. And the more the team members can be themselves. And this will liberate energy, joy and connectedness. This, if anything, gives hope, power and meaning. And better results!

8. If you ever feel you have been accused of something, take a deep breath and try the Seven Golden Words. Say to yourself: *'There is something in what you say.'*

9. Read often: *'I am not upset for the reason I think.'*

Think often: *'What is happening is happening so that I can learn something.'*

10. Choose humility by practising your listening.

Feel free to copy this list

Absolutely true

This is the end of Part Two, with one simple reminder.

You are going to meet other people.

You are going out, perhaps to give a talk or lecture, or maybe to show something, teach something, give someone a treatment . . . or simply just to meet other people . . .

Maybe you are nervous. Try slowly to internalise these thoughts while seeing 'them' — the other people — in front of you.

These thoughts are calming. They are perfectly true.

Say to yourself:

'There is nobody here who is more than anybody else and there is nobody here who is less than anybody else.'

If that thought doesn't help, try this one as well, very slowly:

'There is nobody here from whom I have nothing to learn.'

Each encounter with another person is an opportunity to grow. It is an opportunity to learn more about yourself. Try seeing others as having been sent for your practice.

'The personality only develops through contact with another personality. This mutual awakening and lightening of thought and thought, of will and will is the only, eternal, obvious wonder in our life.'

(Swedish poet Erik Gustav Geijer)

Part 3

'The Graduate Course'

Read this 'graduate course' only when you feel
comfortable with everything you have read so far.

Good luck!

Fear — love

You have already come a long way in this course. What follows now may seem very confusing, or may already be perfectly obvious.

Savour slowly the following wonderful thought:

What if there are only two ways of relating to other people? The one out of fear — the other out of love. These two can never be 'mixed'.

That is to say:

What if everything that isn't love is fear? And everything that isn't fear is love?

Examine the thought slowly. Read it over and over again.

Either I behave towards my surroundings out of a feeling of fear or I do it out of love. There is no other alternative.

Love always implies some form of uniting. A movement towards. Fear always implies some form of separation. A movement away.

For me it has become clear that this is how it is.

Examine the thought. When you feel it is true, you will look at your surroundings in quite a new way.

What, then, if it is also true that:

Every thought, word or deed of mine is

either

an expression of my will to create more unity, more acceptance, more tolerance — that is, more love — in this world

or

an expression of fear — that is, an appeal for love, a cry for help. Love me!

And there is nothing in between.

We all oscillate between these two. Sometimes we exude love and sometimes we seek love.

Live with that thought. Try it. It will become very exciting.

The sacred moment

I have gradually come to believe that this is true:

Fear and love can never be experienced at the same time.

If I am experiencing fear inside, I cannot experience love.

There are only two ways of relating to other people. The one is out of fear — the other is out of love. The two can never be mixed.

Everyone has experience of encounters based on fear. Everyone has felt the tension, the stomach cramps . . . the exhaustion afterwards. Everyone can remember all the thousand different decisions made out of fear . . . and all the regret that followed . . . and so on.

We all also have experience of encounters without fear!

We all have at some time experienced meeting another person completely without fear. Such an encounter between two or more, where all are free of fear, is — every time it happens — *a sacred moment.*

When you are present at such a meeting and really feel that you are fearless, then you experience a warm current of love. For both yourself and your surroundings. You are in contact with what you are meant to be. *Your True Self.*

You feel, too, that you understand the real meaning of these words: *'This present moment — now — is the only time there is.'* The 'Now' has arrived!

In the Now, liberated from fear, everyone feels love.

Harry Martinson* describes such a meeting:

---

* Harry Martinson is a Swedish Nobel prizewinner for literature.

Only rarely can each one of us come to know
a few clear seconds of oblivion and encounter
all swept aside
silent stands the miracle and stares us in the eyes.

Just imagine: can it be that my own inner fear keeps the love in me trapped inside?

Try carrying this thought around with you:

There are only two ways to approach another person.
The one, with fear. The other, with love.

Fear and love can never be experienced simultaneously.

Two fundamental needs

One way to approach real seeing — that is, coming closer to a seeing that perceives the truth — is to keep these words in mind:

**Other people are either givers of love
or fearful people asking for love.**

Memorise those words. Keep them with you in your everyday life. See others as givers of love or as fearful people in need of help, that is love. There is no other kind.

Practise and practise.

You will succeed!

What now follows helps me to understand more easily and to internalise the above:

Human beings have two fundamental needs. On the one hand: **the need to be loved.** And on the other hand a much more primal need: **the need to express love.**

This picture helps me to remember this:

So you can regard other people as love-givers or as frightened love-seekers. That is all there is.

As best I can

Perhaps you have heard or read this sentence sometime:

At any given moment all human beings do the best they can, to the best of their ability, just at that time.

Not necessarily the best they know, but the best they are able, to the best of their ability, at that moment.

What if that is true?

What if that is really true?

Do you find it hard to accept that idea? Can you immediately name some people around you who you think definitely should pull themselves together? I know that feeling well myself, but still . . . give it a go . . . give that sentence a chance for a little while.

Examine the possible truth in the sentence by applying it to a very small child. Why not an infant? Why not yourself when you were very tiny? Why not a foetus lying in a woman's womb?

Every little child at every given moment does the best it can, to the best of its ability, at that moment.

For me this is totally true and feels immensely liberating.

Every little child always does the best it can, to the best of its ability, at any given moment. All else is an expression of my own misinterpretation.

From this follows (logically) that all condemnation, accusation, ridicule, irony aimed at children is in fact a cry for help from the adult. It is a message that I (the adult) am not feeling very well at the moment. That I am under stress. I am disturbed, irritated, off balance. What happens is an example of me projecting my own problems onto someone who is innocent. Everything is projection by the adult.

I don't say it's easy. Most of us were not seen through such eyes as children. We were not seen as doing the best we could.

What if a change could begin with me often telling myself: *'Every child always does the best it can.'*

Then imagine if it might not also be true that:

All human beings, at any given moment, do the best they can, to the best of their ability at that moment.

WHAT IF THAT IS TRUE?

I have been thinking about this for years on and off. Sometimes I have been certain that this is how it is, and then I have become uncertain again.

But one thing I have noticed.

When I look at myself and all my own 'shortcomings' I can, today, say that in all instances I really did the best I could — at that moment. And it feels remarkably liberating to be able to say that to oneself.

You feel that you are looking at yourself with tenderness and real acceptance. The other alternative is to think: *'I could have done better. I should have pulled myself together. Boy! was I stupid!'* In other words, you make yourself feel guilty.

All such emotions imply a punishing and judgemental view of yourself. Which makes you neither healthy nor joyful nor any better!

I would rather believe that it is so: that people always do the best they can. That changes a lot — particularly when I'm about to become irritated at someone. If only I manage to think the thought first: *'Right now she is doing the best she can. Even if it is awfully difficult to see and accept what she does.'*

If I manage to think that thought, it liberates me quite remarkably from a large part of my irritation.

Try it. Practise!

Before difficult encounters

Here is something to read to yourself now and then:

I see the arrogance (the shield . . . the mask . . . the veil)
that you have learned to protect yourself with,
and learned to conceal your fear with.
It is a cry for help.

I see the irony (the shield . . . the mask . . . the veil)
that you have learned to protect yourself with,
and learned to conceal your fear with.
It is a cry for help.

I see the double messages (the mask . . . the game)
that you have learned to protect yourself with,
and learned to conceal your fear with.
They are a cry for help.

I see the hardness, toughness and coldness
    (the mask . . . the shield)
that you have learned to protect yourself with
    in many situations,
and with which you have learned to conceal your fear.
Everything is an appeal for help! A cry for love.

I see the pedantry, the order, the compulsions,
    the manic habits
that you have learned to protect yourself with
    to survive so many chaotic situations,
and with which you then learned to conquer your fear.
They are appeals for help.

I see the silence, muteness, apathy, paralysis,
    all this 'falseness'
that you have learned to enter into,
    probably even as a very small child,

in order to survive numerous difficult and humiliating
    situations,
and which you then have learned to use as a shield
    to hide your fear.
They are cries for help.

My lesson is to see that cry.

Let me practise not to despise it, not to strike out at it, not
to attack and ridicule it, each time I encounter it outside
myself.

It is so easily done because I don't accept it in myself. It
is so easily done because I, too, have all this, or parts of
it, inside me and am doing my best to suppress it.

Life — death

In many ways this entire course is about health.

Read and contemplate:

One big social health research project has become almost a classic. It was carried out by Minnesota University, and it followed 1059 people for more than 25 years.

At the start, they were all 19 years old — a broad sample of male and female, fat and slim, black and white, rich and poor, etc. Much effort went into finding as representative a selection of the population as possible.

These 19-year-olds were charted in different ways, and with utmost care those individuals were also identified who could be called

HIGH FOE-CREATING INDIVIDUALS

Effort was taken to identify those who thought they saw enemies everywhere, in all kinds of situations.

Those individuals were also identified whom one could call:

LOW FOE-CREATING INDIVIDUALS

These 19-year-olds were observed for a quarter of a century!

And they found that: people who see enemies everywhere had a more than

four times greater risk of heart infarction

and had more than

six times higher mortality

A final review

So, see other people as love-givers or as frightened love-seekers.

This is **really to see**. It is also one of the foundations of this course. This is a paraphrase of an earlier sentence in this book:

Every action of mine expresses either a desire to create more love in this world or a request, an appeal, a cry for help: love me.

There are no other alternatives.

See other people as givers of love
or as frightened people asking for love.

You get a chance to practise this in every encounter with another person.

Other people are either givers of love, or frightened people asking for help — that is, asking for love.

Transferred to a relationship the thought could be put like this:

Every action of mine towards a colleague, patient, client, pupil, is either GIVING, with the basic aim of healing that person — that is, giving love. Or it is an expression of the fact that I have a problem that I'm working on, and so I'm asking for help.

Regard relationships as ways for us to work on our development. **Try to look at relationships as missions.**

In each relationship, at every moment, we are teaching either love or fear. In a relationship you can find faults everywhere. It is quite easy, if that is what you are looking for. And you can find good attempts, longing, will, caring and cries for help, if that is what you are looking for.

This always applies

This always applies.

There are only two kinds of reaction, two kinds of facial expression, laughter, voice, phrase and body posture: either they are expressions of love or they are a plea for love.

The laughter you hear is either an expression of love or it expresses a plea for love. The voice you hear is either an expression of love or it expresses a plea for love. The body posture or face are either expressing love or they are a plea for love. Your words and gestures either express love or they plead for love.

This is the lesson we are here to learn.

And so we come to the end of this course.

Thank you for reading these pages.

I wish you all the best.

Guidebooks for Growth Together

is a new collection of books (all at £5.95/US$10.95) launched by Findhorn Press in spring 1995. It consists of books addressed both to individuals and to groups who are looking for practical tools to help them on their spiritual path. To date, this collection includes:

THE ART OF PSYCHIC PROTECTION
Judy Hall (author of The Karmic Journey)

A book of practical techniques and help for any individual or group seeking to expand their consciousness who need to protect themselves from psychic intrusion. For those who meditate, use guided imagery or self-hypnosis tapes, for therapists and healers, for those who find excessive tiredness a problem, the chances are that these people need to protect themselves with these tried and tested tools, some of which date back thousands of years whilst others belong to the 21st century. We protect ourselves in so many ways, we have tended to forget that psychic protection is a basic need.

Pbk 144 pages ISBN 1 899171 36 3

WAVES OF SPIRIT
Practical Ways to Face Today's Life Challenges
Eileen Caddy

The author of *Opening Doors Within*, which has sold over 500,000 copies worldwide in 16 different languages, has produced something completely new. Whereas all her previous books have been based on her guidance received in meditation over the past 40 years, this book is all Eileen the woman: her wisdom and experience learned through hard knocks and struggles in her life. Eileen shares her perspectives on many of life's questions and challenges —forgiveness, unconditional love, healing relationships, sexuality, children and the Christ amongst them. She also answers questions frequently asked by people seeking to find their spiritual path, and offers guided meditations to enable readers to move into the stillness of their own being and find their own inner voice and guidance.

Waves of Spirit will be like a breath of fresh air to all seekers on the spiritual path, particularly the confused and hopeless trying to make sense of life today. Eileen's simple faith and obedience to her inner voice has guided her life and inspired millions of other seekers. This book will doubtless continue her work well into the 21st century.

Pbk   144 pages   ISBN 1 899171 75 4

PLAYFUL SELF-DISCOVERY
A Findhorn Foundation Approach to Building Trust in Groups
David Earl Platts

For more than 15 years, thousands of people have experienced Group Discovery at the Findhorn Foundation. Many of them find the experience the high point of their time there. Now, in this book, we are able to share the strategy underlying Group Discovery with the wider world. *Playful Self-Discovery* is a practical 'how to' book which establishes a group consciousness framework, gives guidelines to enable the reader to lead sessions designed to coalesce a group and provides specific instructions for presenting fifty different Group Discovery Games and exercises.

This book will be of invaluable help and support to group leaders in all walks of life — in schools, churches, centres — and also to social workers, managers and management consultants, as well as workshop leaders and trainers.

Pbk   128 pages   ISBN 1 899171 06 1

affix
stamp
here

to:
Findhorn Press
The Press Building
The Park
Findhorn
Forres IV36 0TZ
Scotland

from: _____

_____

Please
write your
name and
address here   _____

_____

(please
PRINT)   _____

_____

FIND**HORN**
Press

Tel +44 (0)1309 690582
Fax +44 (0)1309 690036
e-mail thierry@findhorn.org
http://www.findhorn.org/findhornpress/

Thank you for choosing this book. We appreciate your interest and support.

If you would like to receive our full catalogue of books and other inspirational material, please fill in this card and mail it to us.

❑   Please send book and music catalogue

❑   Please send information about the Findhorn Foundation

In which book did you find this card? _____

Where did you buy this book? _____

Do you have any special interests? _____

I CLOSE MY EYES AND SEE
Vision for the Inner Journey
Dorothy Lewis

This is a resource book, containing over fifty visualisation exercises. It is intended both for the individual looking for practical help on the inner journey, and for the therapist or group leader who needs more material to use with clients or groups.

The main focus of this book is to help people find or re-find their spiritual roots, and ensuing strength and creativity. In this it differs from the usual motive of personal growth or healing, though these aspects are necessarily included.

It is deliberately written in simple anecdotal style, and is immensely practical, using well-tried material. It is a 'treasury' for group leaders wanting to deepen the experience of their clients or groups.

Pbk   176 pages   ISBN 1 899171 11 8

THE PATH TO LOVE IS THE PRACTICE OF LOVE
An Introduction to Spirituality, with Self-Help Exercises for Small Groups
Carol Riddell

This books explains the meaning of a spiritual life, and provides a way for people to get together with like-minded friends to practise its principles. Through understanding and practice, there is the chance to transform daily life, to give meaning to its experiences, and to find happiness in the service of others. The teachings can apply equally to Christians, Buddhists, Moslems, Hindus or Humanists, as long as it is accepted that the essential principle of the cosmos is love, a love both detached and personal, all-pervasive and specific.

The guidance in this book is 'channelled', a technique for accessing a higher wisdom that can be learned (first third of the book). The exercises have been tested out over a period of four years in workshops in several European countries and at the Findhorn Foundation. Several self-help groups have already used them as a basis (last two thirds of the book).

About the author: Carol Riddell lectured in Sociology at Strathclyde and Lancaster Universities until 1978, after which she studied healing, clairvoyance and herbalism. She was a member of the Findhorn Community between 1983 and 1993, and is now living in Fionnphort on the Isle of Mull where she founded the Highland Renewal Project, a viable exemplary rural community focusing on the promotion of education, research, public awareness and understanding of rural regeneration in the Scottish Highlands.

Pbk   144 pages   ISBN 1 899171 20 7

JOURNEYS WITHIN
Source Book of Guided Meditations
Lisa Davis

This books is aimed at both individuals and groups needing help with guided meditations, and gives the reader support in how to begin, conduct and end meditations. It offers the opportunity to choose a topic from a variety of subjects, such as healing, tarot, colour and the four elements, which can then be recorded and used as required. It is ideal for anyone who is new to guided meditations or who has ever felt insecure or hesitant about leading them. It also gives the opportunity for experienced meditators to expand their repertoire.

About the author: Lisa Davis is a management consultant, trainer and writer of teaching and learning materials. She also runs a spiritual development group and enjoys working with sound and healing energy.

Pbk   144 pages   ISBN 1 899171 35 5